Mexican Food

Discover Authentic Mexican Food with Delicious Mexican Recipes

By
BookSumo Press

Published by
http://www.booksumo.com

LEGAL NOTES

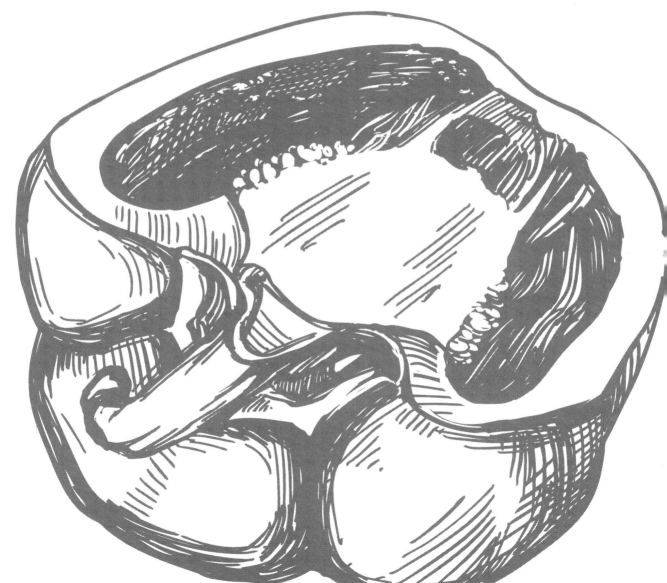

Table of Contents

Party Quesadillas

Prep Time: 30 mins
Total Time: 55 mins

Servings per Recipe: 20

Calories	244 kcal
Fat	11.3 g
Carbohydrates	21.8g
Protein	13.7 g
Cholesterol	35 mg
Sodium	504 mg

Ingredients

1 lb. skinless, boneless chicken breast, diced
1 (1.27 oz.) packet fajita seasoning
1 tbsp vegetable oil
2 green bell peppers, chopped
2 red bell peppers, chopped
1 onion, chopped

10 (10 inch) flour tortillas
1 (8 oz.) package shredded Cheddar cheese
1 tbsp bacon bits
1 (8 oz.) package shredded Monterey Jack cheese

Directions

1. Set the broiler of your oven and grease a baking sheet.
2. In a bowl, add the chicken and fajita seasoning and toss to coat.
3. Place chicken pieces onto the baking sheet.
4. Cook under the broiler for about 5 minutes.
5. Now, set your oven to 350 degrees F.
6. In a large pan, heat the oil on medium heat and sauté the green bell peppers, red bell peppers, onion and chicken for about 10 minutes.
7. Place the chicken mixture over the tortilla and sprinkle with the Cheddar cheese, followed by the bacon bits and Monterey Jack.
8. Fold the tortillas in half and Place onto a baking sheet.
9. Cook in the oven for about 10 minutes.

SEAFOOD
Quesadillas

🥘 Prep Time: 15 mins
🕐 Total Time: 1 hr 15 mins

Servings per Recipe: 6	
Calories	753 kcal
Fat	36.9 g
Carbohydrates	67.8g
Protein	37.9 g
Cholesterol	180 mg
Sodium	1788 mg

Ingredients

2 tbsp vegetable oil
1 onion, sliced
1 red bell pepper, sliced
1 green bell pepper, sliced
1 tsp salt
1 tsp ground cumin
1 tsp chili powder
1 lb. uncooked medium shrimp, peeled and deveined

1 jalapeno pepper, seeded and minced
1 lime, juiced
1 tsp vegetable oil
6 large flour tortillas
3 C. shredded Mexican cheese blend, divided

Directions

1. In a large skillet, heat 2 tbsp of the vegetable oil on medium-high heat and sauté the onion, red bell pepper and green bell pepper for about 6-8 minutes.
2. Stir in the salt, cumin and chili powder.
3. Stir in the shrimp and cook for about 3-5 minutes.
4. Remove the skillet from the heat and stir in the jalapeño pepper and lime juice.
5. In a skillet, heat 1 tsp of the oil on medium heat.
6. Place a tortilla in the hot oil.
7. Place about 1/6 shrimp filling and 1/2 C. Mexican cheese blend on one side of tortilla.
8. Fold the tortilla in half.
9. Cook for about 5 minutes
10. Carefully, flip the side and cook for about 3-5 minutes.
11. Repeat with remaining tortillas and filling.

Family Favorite
Quesadilla Burgers

Prep Time: 20 mins
Total Time: 30 mins

Servings per Recipe: 4	
Calories	1192 kcal
Fat	77 g
Carbohydrates	163g
Protein	61 g
Cholesterol	1217 mg
Sodium	1810 mg

Ingredients

Southwest Sauce:
1/2 C. sour cream
1/4 C. ranch dressing
1/4 C. taco sauce
4 (4 oz.) hamburger patties
1 dash Worcestershire sauce
8 flour tortillas

2 C. shredded sharp Cheddar cheese
2 C. shredded Colby-Jack cheese
1/2 head lettuce, shredded
3 tbsp picante sauce

Directions

1. In a bowl, add the sour cream, ranch dressing and taco sauce and mix till sauce mixture becomes smooth.
2. Refrigerate, covered for flavors to blend.
3. Set your outdoor grill for medium-high heat and grease the grill grate.
4. Cook hamburger patties on the grill for about 5 minutes, seasoning with the Worcestershire sauce.
5. Flip the patties and place the tortillas on the grill and set the grill to medium-low under the tortillas.
6. Add Cheddar cheese and Colby-Jack cheese to tortillas and grill for about 2-4 minutes.
7. Cooking the hamburger patties for about 5 minutes more.
8. Spread Southwest sauce onto 1/2 of the tortillas and top with the lettuce and picante sauce.
9. Place 1 hamburger patty on top of picante sauce and top patty with a tortilla, making a sandwich.

STEAK
Quesadillas

Prep Time: 10 mins
Total Time: 25 mins

Servings per Recipe: 4
Calories	552 kcal
Fat	31.1 g
Carbohydrates	40g
Protein	28 g
Cholesterol	79 mg
Sodium	762 mg

Ingredients

2 tbsp vegetable oil, divided
1/2 onion, sliced
1/2 green bell pepper, sliced
salt to taste
4 flour tortillas

1/2 lb. cooked steak, cut into 1/4-inch thick pieces
1 C. shredded Mexican cheese blend

Directions

1. In a 10-inch skillet, heat 2 tsp of the oil on medium heat and sauté the onion and green bell pepper for about 5-10 minutes.
2. Stir in the salt and transfer the mixture into a bowl.
3. Brush 1 side of each tortilla with the remaining oil.
4. Place 1 tortilla, oil-side down, in the same skillet and sprinkle with 1/2 of the steak, 1/2 of the onion mixture and 1/2 of the Mexican cheese mixture.
5. Place a second tortilla, oil-side up, on top, pressing down with a spatula to seal.
6. Cook the quesadilla over medium heat for about 3-4 minutes per side.
7. Remove the quesadilla from skillet and cut into wedges.
8. Repeat with the remaining ingredients for second quesadilla.

Quesadillas
Tegucigalpa Style

Prep Time: 25 mins
Total Time: 2 hrs 10 mins

Servings per Recipe: 16
Calories   515 kcal
Fat   23.4 g
Carbohydrates   68g
Protein   9.9 g
Cholesterol   73 mg
Sodium   478 mg

Ingredients

1 1/2 C. margarine
3 C. white sugar
2 C. sifted all-purpose flour
1 C. rice flour
1 tbsp baking powder
6 room-temperature eggs
2 C. lukewarm milk

2 C. grated Parmesan cheese
1/2 C. white sugar
1/4 C. all-purpose flour
1/4 C. sesame seeds

Directions

1. Set your oven to 350 degrees F before doing anything else and lightly grease and flour a medium glass baking dish.
2. In a bowl, add the margarine and 3 C. of the sugar and beat till fluffy.
3. Add the eggs one at a time, mixing till well combined.
4. In another bowl, mix together 2 C. of the all-purpose flour, rice flour and baking powder.
5. Slowly, add the flour mixture into the egg mixture alternately with the milk, stirring well between each addition.
6. Slowly stir in the Parmesan cheese and transfer the mixture into the prepared baking dish.
7. In a small bowl, mix together 1/2 C. of the sugar, 1/4 C. of the all-purpose flour and sesame seeds.
8. Sprinkle evenly over the mixture in the baking dish.
9. Cook in the oven for about 45 minutes or till a toothpick inserted in the center comes out clean.
10. Cool completely and cut into squares.

CREAMY
Chicken Dinner

Prep Time: 15 mins
Total Time: 45 mins

Servings per Recipe: 4

Calories	505 kcal
Fat	23.7 g
Carbohydrates	42.8g
Protein	30.8 g
Cholesterol	131 mg
Sodium	368 mg

Ingredients

1 cup couscous
1 1/8 cups boiling chicken stock
water to cover
2 tablespoons butter
4 skinless, boneless chicken breast
halves
2/3 cup heavy whipping cream
1/2 cup sweet corn
2 tomatoes, chopped

1/4 cup fresh chopped tarragon
salt and pepper to taste
1/2 lemon, juiced

Directions

1. Add your couscous to a pot then pour in half of the chicken stock and then pour in water to submerge everything. Place a lid on the pot. Get the mix hot and boiling for about 4 mins then shut the heat.

2. Get your butter bubbly in a frying pan then begin to stir fry your chicken breasts in it. Add the other half of the chicken stock and also the cream. Get everything simmering then once it is combine in your tomatoes, half of the tarragon, and the corn. Stir everything completely then let the mix cook for 60 secs. Now add in your pepper and salt and stir everything again.

3. Stir your couscous then add some lemon juice and bunch of tarragon. Add some pepper and salt then divide the couscous between serving dishes and top each liberally with your chicken and garnish everything with some additional tarragon.

4. Enjoy.

Light
Mexican Corn Stir Fry

🥄 Prep Time: 15 mins
🕐 Total Time: 40 mins

Servings per Recipe: 3	
Calories	331 kcal
Fat	17.9 g
Carbohydrates	32.6g
Protein	16 g
Cholesterol	50 mg
Sodium	421 mg

Ingredients

3 ears corn, husked and cleaned
1 tablespoon butter
1 onion, diced
3 small zucchini, cut into 1/4-inch slices
3 small yellow summer squash, cut into

1/4-inch slices
salt and pepper to taste
1 cup lightly packed shredded Cheddar cheese

Directions

1. Get your corn boiling in a pot for 5 mins. Then place everything into a cool water.

2. Get your butter hot in a frying pan then begin to fry your onion in the butter for 6 mins. Combine in the corn and let it cook for 6 mins then combine in the pieces of squash and the zucchini. Set the heat to low and place a lid on the frying pan.

3. Let everything cook for 10 mins. Take off the lid and top everything with some pepper, salt, and cheddar cheese. Place the lid back on the pan and shut the heat let everything set until the cheese is melted nicely.

4. Enjoy.

TEX-MEX
Pasta

Prep Time: 25 mins
Total Time: 45 mins

Servings per Recipe: 6
Calories	508 kcal
Fat	20.2 g
Carbohydrates	59.9g
Protein	23.7 g
Cholesterol	163 mg
Sodium	593 mg

Ingredients

1 (16 ounce) package linguine pasta
1 pound peeled and deveined medium shrimp
1 tablespoon liquid shrimp and crab boil seasoning
1/2 cup butter
1 teaspoon minced garlic
1/3 cup diced red onion
1/3 cup diced sweet red bell pepper
1/2 cup canned whole kernel corn, drained

1 1/2 tablespoons fresh lime juice
2 tablespoons chopped fresh cilantro
1 teaspoon dried oregano
1 teaspoon canned chipotle chili peppers in adobo sauce, finely chopped
1 teaspoon sea salt
1/2 cup half-and-half

Directions

1. Get your pasta boiling in the water with salt for 9 mins then remove the liquids.

2. Get a 2nd pot for your crab boil and shrimp and get everything submerged under water. Let the shrimp boil for 5 mins then remove the liquid.

3. Now get your butter hot in a frying pan then begin to stir fry your red onion, and garlic for 5 mins then combine in the salt, bell pepper, chipotle pepper, corn, oregano, cilantro, and lime juice. Now add in the half and half and get everything lightly boiling.

4. Once the mix is gently simmering add in the shrimp and then the pasta and toss everything evenly.

5. Enjoy.

How to Make
Corn Chowder

🥣 Prep Time: 15 mins
🕐 Total Time: 35 mins

Servings per Recipe: 6
Calories	420 kcal
Fat	19.3 g
Carbohydrates	40.7g
Protein	24.1 g
Cholesterol	204 mg
Sodium	366 mg

Ingredients

2 tablespoons butter
2 leeks (white and pale green parts only), chopped
salt and ground black pepper to taste
2 tablespoons all-purpose flour
3 cups half-and-half
1 pound potatoes, peeled and chopped

1 (8 ounce) bottle clam juice
1 pound cooked shrimp
2 (8 ounce) bags frozen corn
2 tablespoons fresh lemon juice
2 tablespoons chopped fresh chives

Directions

1. Get your butter hot in a heavy pot, like the Dutch oven.
2. Once the butter is hot add in your pepper, salt, and leeks. Let the leeks fry in the butter for 7 mins.
3. Add your flour to leek mix while stirring everything and let the mix get thick then combine in the clam juice, half and half, and potatoes.
4. Get everything boiling then once it is boiling, set the heat to low, and let everything cook for 12 mins.
5. Combine the corn and shrimp into the mix then let everything continue to cook for 12 more mins.
6. Shut the heat and combine in your chives and lemon juice.
7. Enjoy.

SIMPLE
Corn Soup

Prep Time: 15 mins
Total Time: 45 mins

Servings per Recipe: 4	
Calories	202 kcal
Fat	7.3 g
Carbohydrates	23.3g
Protein	14.9 g
Cholesterol	56 mg
Sodium	139 mg

Ingredients

4 ears fresh corn, shucked and desilked
1 tablespoon olive oil
1 medium onion, chopped
2 cloves garlic, minced
1/4 pound chicken, cubed
1/4 pound uncooked prawns, peeled
and deveined

salt and pepper to taste
4 cups chicken broth
1 bunch fresh spinach, washed and dried

Directions

1. Get a bowl and with a sharp knife carefully remove the corn kernels from your ears of corn. Place all the kernels into the bowl.
2. Get a frying pan hot with olive oil then begin to sit fry your garlic and onion in the oil for 7 mins. Combine in your chicken pieces and fry them until they are fully done for 7 mins then combine in the prawns and cook them for until they are done as well for about 6 to 8 mins more.
3. Now pour in the corn and stir then add in some pepper and salt then stir everything again. Now combine in your chicken broth and get everything gently boiling. Let the mix simmer for 11 mins then combine in the spinach and cook everything for 4 more mins.
4. Enjoy.

Indo-Mexican Style
Basmati Rice

Prep Time: 5 mins
Total Time: 30 mins

Servings per Recipe: 5

Calories	263 kcal
Fat	5.9 g
Carbohydrates	50.4g
Protein	5.7 g
Cholesterol	12 mg
Sodium	36 mg

Ingredients

2 tablespoons butter, divided
1 cup Basmati rice
2 cups water
2 cups fresh corn kernels
3 large shallots, sliced thinly
1/2 teaspoon white sugar
salt to taste

ground black pepper to taste
2 tablespoons chopped fresh mint leaves

Directions

1. Get 1 tbsps of butter hot in a pot then combine in your water and rice. Get everything boiling, then once it is, place a lid on the pot, set the heat to low, and let the rice cook for 17 mins.
2. At the same time get 1 more tbsp of butter hot in a frying pan then combine in the pepper, corn, salt, sugar, and shallots. Stir fry the mix for 5 mins.
3. Get a bowl, combine the rice, mint, and corn mix. Toss everything completely.
4. Enjoy.

SPICY
Mexican Quinoa

Prep Time: 20 mins
Total Time: 40 mins

Servings per Recipe: 4
Calories	244 kcal
Fat	6.1 g
Carbohydrates	38.1g
Protein	8.1 g
Cholesterol	2 mg
Sodium	986 mg

Ingredients

1 tbsp olive oil
1 C. quinoa, rinsed
1 small onion, chopped
2 cloves garlic, minced
1 jalapeno pepper, seeded and chopped
1 (10 oz.) can diced tomatoes with
green chili peppers

1 envelope taco seasoning mix
2 C. low-sodium chicken broth
1/4 C. chopped fresh cilantro

Directions

1. In a large skillet, heat the oil on medium heat and stir fry the quinoa and onion for about 5 minutes.
2. Add the garlic and jalapeño pepper and cook for about 1-2 minutes.
3. Stir in the undrained can of diced tomatoes with green chilis, taco seasoning mix and chicken broth and bring to a boil.
4. Reduce the heat to medium-low and simmer for about 15-20 minutes.
5. Stir in cilantro and serve.

South of the Border Style Pesto

Prep Time: 10 mins
Total Time: 10 mins

Servings per Recipe: 6
Calories	176 kcal
Fat	17.8 g
Cholesterol	2.4g
Sodium	2.9 g
Carbohydrates	6 mg
Protein	262 mg

Ingredients

1/4 C. hulled pumpkin seeds (pepitas)
1 bunch cilantro
1/4 C. grated cotija cheese
4 cloves garlic

1 serrano chili pepper, seeded
1/2 tsp salt
6 tbsp olive oil

Directions

1. In a food processor, add the pumpkin seeds and pulse till chopped roughly.
2. Add the remaining ingredients and pulse till smooth.

EL POLLO
Soup

Prep Time: 20 mins
Total Time: 1 hr 5 mins

Servings per Recipe: 4

Calories	335 kcal
Fat	7.7 g
Carbohydrates	37.7g
Protein	31.5 g
Cholesterol	62 mg
Sodium	841 mg

Ingredients

3 cooked, boneless chicken breast
halves, shredded
1 (15 oz.) can kidney beans
1 C. whole kernel corn
1 (14.5 oz.) can stewed tomatoes
1/2 C. chopped onion
1/2 green bell pepper, chopped

1/2 red bell pepper, chopped
1 (4 oz.) can chopped green chili peppers
2 (14.5 oz.) cans chicken broth
1 tbsp ground cumin

Directions

1. In a large pan mix together all the ingredients on medium heat.
2. Simmer for about 45 minutes.

Restaurant-Style
Latin Rice

Prep Time: 20 mins
Total Time: 55 mins

Servings per Recipe: 6
Calories	510 kcal
Fat	18.3 g
Carbohydrates	59.1g
Protein	28.3 g
Cholesterol	74 mg
Sodium	1294 mg

Ingredients

1 lb. lean ground beef
1 onion, diced
1 green bell pepper, diced
1 (14 oz.) can beef broth
2 C. fresh corn kernels
1 (10 oz.) can diced tomatoes with green chili peppers
1 (15 oz.) can tomato sauce
1/2 C. salsa
1/2 tsp chili powder

1/2 tsp paprika
1/2 tsp garlic powder
1/2 tsp salt
1/2 tsp ground black pepper
1 tsp minced cilantro
1 1/2 C. uncooked white rice
1 C. shredded Cheddar cheese

Directions

1. Heat a medium pan on medium heat and cook the beef till browned completely.
2. Drain off the grease from the pan.
3. Add the onion and green pepper and cook till the onion becomes tender.
4. Stir in the beef broth, corn, tomatoes with green chili peppers and tomato sauce, salsa, chili powder, paprika, garlic powder, salt, pepper and cilantro and bring to a boil.
5. Stir in the rice and cook, covered for about 25 minutes.
6. Top with the Cheddar cheese and cook for about 10 minutes.

CANELA
Brownies

Prep Time: 20 mins
Total Time: 1 hr 30 mins

Servings per Recipe: 30
Calories	206 kcal
Fat	10.8 g
Carbohydrates	27g
Protein	2.7 g
Cholesterol	62 mg
Sodium	76 mg

Ingredients

1 1/2 C. unsalted butter
3 C. white sugar
6 eggs
1 tbsp vanilla extract
1 1/4 C. unsweetened cocoa powder
1 3/4 tsp ground Mexican cinnamon
(canela)

1 1/2 C. all-purpose flour
1/2 tsp ground pequin chili pepper
3/4 tsp kosher salt
3/4 tsp baking powder

Directions

1. Set your oven to 350 degrees F before doing anything else and line a 15x12-inch baking dish with the parchment paper, leaving about 3 inches of paper overhanging 2 sides to use as handles.
2. In a microwave-safe bowl, add the butter and microwave on Medium for about 1 minute.
3. Add the sugar and mix till well combined.
4. Add the eggs, one at a time, and mix till well combined.
5. Stir in the vanilla extract.
6. In a bowl, sift together the flour, cocoa, cinnamon, pequin pepper, salt and baking powder.
7. Add the flour mixture into the butter mixture and mix till well combined.
8. Transfer the mixture into the prepared baking dish evenly.
9. Cook in the oven for about 20-25 minutes or till a toothpick inserted into the center comes out clean.
10. Remove from the oven and keep aside to cool in the pan.
11. Remove the parchment paper handles to remove the brownies for slicing.

Ground Beef
Mexican Dip

🥘 Prep Time: 25 mins
🕐 Total Time: 50 mins

Servings per Recipe: 32
Calories   150 kcal
Fat   11.3 g
Carbohydrates   3.9g
Protein   8.3 g
Cholesterol   30 mg
Sodium   429 mg

Ingredients

1 lb. ground beef

1 (16 oz.) jar salsa

1 (10.75 oz.) can condensed cream of mushroom soup

2 lb. processed cheese food, cubed

Directions

1. Heat a medium pan on medium-high heat and cook the beef till browned completely.
2. Drain off the grease from the pan.
3. In a slow cooker, transfer the cooked beef with the salsa, condensed cream of mushroom soup and processed cheese food.
4. Set the slow cooker on High till cheese melts completely.
5. Now, set the slow cooker on Low and simmer till serving.

A STRONG COFFEE
in Mexico

Prep Time: 5 mins
Total Time: 5 mins

Servings per Recipe: 32
Calories	150 kcal
Fat	11.3 g
Cholesterol	3.9g
Sodium	8.3 g
Carbohydrates	30 mg
Protein	429 mg

Ingredients

1 sugar cube
1 fluid oz. hot water
3/4 C. coffee
1 fluid oz. coffee-flavored liqueur

1 tbsp whipped cream

Directions

1. In a coffee mug, add the sugar and hot water.
2. Stir in the coffee and liqueur and top with the whipped cream.

Quick
Midweek Mexican Macaroni

🍲 Prep Time: 20 mins
🕐 Total Time: 50 mins

Servings per Recipe: 8
Calories	374 kcal
Fat	21.4 g
Carbohydrates	23.5g
Protein	22.9 g
Cholesterol	79 mg
Sodium	997 mg

Ingredients

1 C. dry macaroni
1 lb. ground beef
1 small onion, chopped
1 (11 oz.) can whole kernel corn, drained

1 (10 oz.) can diced tomatoes with green chili peppers, drained
1 (1 lb.) loaf processed cheese, cubed

Directions

1. In large pan of the boiling water, add the macaroni for about 8 minutes.
2. Drain well.
3. Meanwhile, heat a medium skillet on medium-high heat and cook the beef till browned completely.
4. Add the onion and cook till browned.
5. Drain off the grease from the skillet.
6. Reduce the heat to medium and stir in the corn, tomatoes, cheese and cooked noodles.
7. Cook, stirring gently till bubbly.

GROUND TURKEY
Queso Enchiladas

Prep Time: 20 mins
Total Time: 1 hr

Servings per Recipe: 7
Calories	414 kcal
Fat	18.5 g
Carbohydrates	30.9g
Protein	29.1 g
Cholesterol	84 mg
Sodium	1341 mg

Ingredients

1 lb. lean ground turkey
2 large carrots, grated
2 tbsp dried minced onion
1 diced fresh jalapeno pepper
1 (1.25 oz.) package taco seasoning mix
1/2 tsp kosher salt
1/4 C. water
hot garlic-pepper sauce
1 C. plain Greek yogurt

1 (10.75 oz.) can condensed cream of chicken soup
2 C. shredded queso quesadilla (Mexican melting cheese)
7 (6 inch) flour tortillas
1/2 (14.5 oz.) can red enchilada sauce

Directions

1. Set your oven to 350 degrees F before doing anything else.
2. Heat a large skillet on medium-high heat and cook the gourd turkey, onions, carrots, jalapeño, 1/2 packet of the taco seasoning and salt till the turkey is browned completely.
3. Stir in the water, several dashes of the hot sauce and the remaining taco seasoning and simmer till the water is absorbed.
4. In a bowl, mix together the yogurt, cream of chicken soup and queso quesadilla cheese.
5. Place a tortilla onto a smooth surface and place some of the turkey mixture halfway between the bottom edge and the center of the tortilla.
6. Place 2-3 tbsp of the cheese mixture over the turkey mixture and roll the tortilla up to the top edge, forming a tight cylinder.
7. Arrange the tortillas in an 11x7-inch baking dish.
8. Repeat with the remaining ingredients.
9. Mix together the enchilada sauce and the remaining cheese mixture.
10. Place the mixture over the top of the tortillas evenly and cook in the oven for about 30-35 minutes.

Azteca
Enchiladas

Azteca

🥄 Prep Time: 30 mins
🕐 Total Time: 1 hr

Servings per Recipe: 9
Calories	284 kcal
Fat	20.3 g
Carbohydrates	17.1g
Protein	11 g
Cholesterol	70 mg
Sodium	222 mg

Ingredients

2 cloves garlic
3 serrano peppers
1 lb. small green tomatillos, husks removed
1 C. vegetable oil for frying
9 corn tortillas
3 C. water
4 tsp chicken bouillon granules
1/2 store-bought rotisserie chicken, meat removed and shredded

1/4 head iceberg lettuce, shredded
1 C. cilantro leaves
1 (8 oz.) container Mexican crema, crema Fresca
1 C. grated cotija cheese

Directions

1. With a foil paper, cover a large griddle and preheat to medium-high heat.
2. Cook the garlic for about 5 minutes, Serrano peppers for about 10 minutes and tomatillos for about 15 minutes.
3. Transfer the vegetables into a bowl and keep aside to cool.
4. In a small, deep skillet, heat the oil to 350 degrees F.
5. With the kitchen tongs, fry the tortillas, one by one for about 5 seconds per side.
6. Transfer the tortillas onto a paper towel lined plate to drain and keep warm.
7. In a blender, place the toasted garlic, Serrano peppers, tomatillos, and water and pulse till smooth.
8. Transfer the mixture into a pan on medium heat and bring to a boil.
9. Dissolve the chicken bouillon into the mixture and reduce the heat to medium-low.
10. Simmer for about 10 minutes.
11. Soak three tortillas in the sauce, one at a time for a few seconds.
12. Fill the tortillas with the shredded chicken and drizzle with some of the sauce.
13. Roll the tortillas and in a pasta bowl, place them seam side down.

14. Place a generous amount of the sauce over the tortillas and top them with the lettuce, cilantro, crema, and cotija cheese.
15. Pour a little more sauce over the whole thing if desired.
16. Repeat the procedure twice more.
17. Serve immediately.

Authentic
Mexican Enchiladas

🥣 Prep Time: 45 mins

🕐 Total Time: 1 hr 5 mins

Servings per Recipe: 6

Calories	737 kcal
Fat	52.1 g
Carbohydrates	42.3g
Protein	28.5 g
Cholesterol	136 mg
Sodium	977 mg

Ingredients

2 tbsp butter
2/3 C. chopped Spanish onion
2 tbsp all-purpose flour
1 1/2 C. chicken broth
1 C. chopped green chili peppers
1 clove garlic, minced
3/4 tsp salt
1 dash ground cumin
12 (8 inch) corn tortillas
canola oil for frying
1 C. shredded Monterey Jack cheese
1 C. shredded mild Cheddar cheese
2 C. shredded, cooked chicken breast meat
1 C. heavy cream
1/4 C. chopped green onion
1/2 C. sliced green olives
1 pint cherry tomatoes

Directions

1. Set your oven to 350 degrees F before doing anything else.
2. For the salsa verde in a pan, melt the butter on medium heat and sauté the onion till soft. Slowly, stir in the flour.
3. Add the broth, chilis, garlic, salt, and cumin and simmer for about 15 minutes.
4. In a heavy skillet, lightly fry tortillas in shallow oil, being careful not to make them too crisp to roll.
5. In a bowl, mix together the cheeses and keep 1/2 C. aside for topping.
6. Dip each tortilla in salsa verde from both sides. Place 2 heaping tbsp of the chicken and about 2 tbsp cheese in the center of each tortilla.
7. Roll the tortillas and in a shallow dish, place them, seam side down. Place the additional salsa verde over the tortillas and then cover with the heavy cream evenly.
8. Sprinkle with remaining 1/2 C. of the cheese mixture and with the green onions.
9. Cook in the oven for about 20 minutes.
10. Serve immediately with a garnishing of the olives, cherry tomatoes, and with additional salsa on the side.

HOMEMADE
Enchilada Sauce

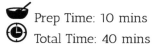

Prep Time: 10 mins
Total Time: 40 mins

Servings per Recipe: 12
Calories	43 kcal
Fat	2.2 g
Carbohydrates	6.1g
Protein	1 g
Cholesterol	0 mg
Sodium	35 mg

Ingredients

1 tbsp vegetable oil
1 C. diced onion
3 tbsp chopped garlic
1 tsp dried oregano
1 tsp ground cumin
1/4 tsp ground cinnamon
3 tbsp all-purpose flour

5 tbsp hot chili powder
4 1/2 C. chicken broth
1/2 (1 oz.) square semisweet chocolate

Directions

1. In a large pan, heat the oil on medium-high high heat and sauté the onion till soft.
2. Stir in the garlic, oregano, cumin and cinnamon and sauté for a few minutes.
3. Stir in the flour and chili powder, stirring until sauce becomes thick.
4. Slowly stir in the chicken broth and simmer till the sauce reaches desired consistency.
5. Stir in the chocolate till melts and well combined.

Cream of Chicken
Enchiladas

Prep Time: 15 mins
Total Time: 30 mins

Servings per Recipe: 6
Calories	453 kcal
Fat	20.4 g
Carbohydrates	42.3g
Protein	24.7 g
Cholesterol	65 mg
Sodium	1186 mg

Ingredients

2 1/2 C. chopped cooked chicken
1 (10.75 oz.) can condensed cream of chicken soup
1 C. sour cream, divided

1/4 C. chopped cilantro
12 (6 inch) flour tortillas
1 1/2 C. salsa

Directions

1. Set your oven to 350 degrees F before doing anything else and line a baking dish with a greased foil paper.
2. In a bowl, mix together the chicken, soup, half of the sour cream, cheese and cilantro.
3. Place about 1/4 C. of the chicken mixture in the center of each tortilla and roll up.
4. In the prepared place the tortillas, seam sides down.
5. Top with salsa and remaining cheese.
6. Cover with the foil and cook in the oven for about 15 minutes.
7. Uncover and cook in the oven for about 10 minutes.
8. Serve with a topping of the cilantro and sour cream.

CINNAMON
x Apple Enchiladas

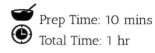
Prep Time: 10 mins
Total Time: 1 hr

Servings per Recipe: 6
Calories	530 kcal
Fat	18.9 g
Carbohydrates	88.2g
Protein	4.6 g
Cholesterol	41 mg
Sodium	392 mg

Ingredients

1 (21 oz.) can apple pie filling
6 (8 inch) flour tortillas
1 tsp ground cinnamon
1/2 C. butter
1/2 C. white sugar

1/2 C. brown sugar
1/2 C. water

Directions

1. Grease a large baking dish.
2. Place about 1/4 C. of the pie filling in the center of each tortilla evenly and sprinkle with the cinnamon.
3. Roll the tortillas, tucking in edges and place in the prepared baking dish, seam side down.
4. In a medium pan, mix together the butter, white sugar, brown sugar and water on medium heat and bring to a boil, stirring continuously.
5. Reduce the heat and simmer for about 3 minutes.
6. Place the sauce over the enchiladas and keep aside for about 30 minutes.
7. Set your oven to 350 degrees F.
8. Cook in the oven for about 20 minutes.

Ultimate Enchiladas

🍳 Prep Time: 30 mins
🕐 Total Time: 1 hr 30 mins

Servings per Recipe: 8	
Calories	498 kcal
Fat	15.9 g
Carbohydrates	49.7g
Protein	26.7 g
Cholesterol	72 mg
Sodium	1227 mg

Ingredients

4 skinless, boneless chicken breast halves
1 onion, chopped
1/2 pint sour cream
1 C. shredded Cheddar cheese
1 tbsp dried parsley
1/2 tsp dried oregano
1/2 tsp ground black pepper
1/2 tsp salt
1 (15 oz.) can tomato sauce

1/2 C. water
1 tbsp chili powder
1/3 C. chopped green bell pepper
1 clove garlic, minced
8 (10 inch) flour tortillas
1 (12 oz.) jar taco sauce
3/4 C. shredded Cheddar cheese

Directions

1. Set your oven to 350 degrees F before doing anything else.
2. Heat a medium non-stick skillet on medium heat and cook the chicken till done completely.
3. Drain excess fat from the skillet.
4. Cut the chicken into the cubes and return into the skillet.
5. Add the onion, sour cream, Cheddar cheese, parsley, oregano and ground black pepper and heat till the cheese melts.
6. Stir in the tomato sauce, chili powder, green pepper, garlic, salt and water.
7. Place the chicken mixture in each tortilla evenly.
8. In a 9x13 inch baking dish, place the tortillas and top with the taco sauce and 3/4 C. of the Cheddar cheese.
9. Cook in the oven for about 20 minutes.

OCTOBER'S
Tex Mex Soup

Prep Time: 10 mins
Total Time: 50 mins

Servings per Recipe: 6	
Calories	684 kcal
Fat	30.5 g
Carbohydrates	59.2g
Protein	45.7 g
Cholesterol	112 mg
Sodium	2036 mg

Ingredients

1 tbsp olive oil
1/2 C. minced onion
3 cloves garlic, minced
2 tsp chili powder
1/2 tsp cumin
1/2 tsp oregano
4 C. water
1 (10.75 oz.) can condensed tomato
soup
1 (28 oz.) can diced tomatoes
1 C. salsa
4 C. shredded cooked turkey
1 tbsp dried parsley
3 chicken bouillon cubes
1 (14 oz.) can black beans, rinsed,
drained
2 C. frozen corn
1/2 C. sour cream
1/4 C. chopped fresh cilantro
Toppings:
6 C. corn tortilla chips
3/4 C. chopped green onion
1 C. shredded Cheddar-Monterey Jack
cheese blend
1/2 C. chopped fresh cilantro
1/2 C. sour cream

Directions

1. In a large pan, heat the olive oil on medium heat and sauté the minced onions for about 4 minutes.
2. Add the garlic, chili powder, cumin and oregano and sauté for about 1 minute.
3. Stir in the water, tomato soup, diced tomatoes, salsa, shredded turkey, parsley and bouillon cubes and bring to a boil.
4. Reduce the heat and simmer for about 5 minutes.
5. Add the black beans, corn, sour cream and cilantro and simmer for about 20-30 minutes.
6. Serve the soup with a topping of the crushed tortilla chips, chopped green onion, shredded cheese, additional cilantro and sour cream.

A True
Texan Cake

Prep Time: 30 mins
Total Time: 45 mins

Servings per Recipe: 15
Calories	449 kcal
Fat	22.8 g
Carbohydrates	57.7g
Protein	7 g
Cholesterol	32 mg
Sodium	379 mg

Ingredients

2 C. all-purpose flour
1 1/2 C. brown sugar
1 tsp baking soda
1 tsp ground cinnamon
1/2 tsp salt
1 C. margarine
1 C. water
1/4 C. unsweetened cocoa powder
1 tbsp instant coffee granules
1/3 C. sweetened condensed milk

2 eggs
1 tsp vanilla extract
1/4 C. margarine
1/4 C. unsweetened cocoa powder
1 tbsp instant coffee granules
2/3 C. sweetened condensed milk
1 C. confectioners' sugar
1 C. slivered, toasted almonds

Directions

1. Set your oven to 350 degrees F before doing anything else and grease a 15x10-inch jelly roll pan.

2. In a bowl, mix together the flour, baking soda, brown sugar, cinnamon and salt.

3. In a small pan, melt 1 C. of the margarine. Stir in the water, 1/4 C. of the cocoa and 1 tbsp of the instant coffee and bring to a boil.

4. Remove from the heat.

5. Make a well in the center of the flour mixture. Place the cocoa mixture in the well of the flour mixture. Add 1/3 C. of the sweetened condensed milk, eggs and vanilla and mix till well combined. Transfer the mixture into the prepared pan.

6. Cook in the oven for about 15-20 minutes. Remove from the oven and keep aside to cool.

7. For the coffee glaze in a small pan, melt 1/4 C. of the margarine.

8. Add 1/4 C. of the cocoa, 1 tbsp of the instant coffee and sweetened condensed milk, and confectioners' sugar and stir to combine. Fold in the almonds. Spread the glaze over the warm cake.

TUESDAY'S
San Miguel Potatoes

Prep Time: 10 mins
Total Time: 1 hr

Servings per Recipe: 4
Calories	420 kcal
Fat	13.2 g
Carbohydrates	60.3g
Protein	17.2 g
Cholesterol	25 mg
Sodium	681 mg

Ingredients

4 baking potatoes
1 tbsp vegetable oil
1 onion, chopped
1 large green bell pepper, chopped
1 tsp minced garlic
1 (16 oz.) can chili beans in spicy sauce, undrained

1 tbsp vegetarian Worcestershire sauce
1/2 tsp minced jalapeno peppers
1 C. shredded Monterey Jack cheese

Directions

1. With a sharp knife, scrub the potatoes and prick in several places.
2. Place the potatoes onto a paper towel and arrange in a microwave and microwave on high for about 8 minutes.
3. Turn and rotate the potatoes and microwave for about 8-10 minutes.
4. In a medium skillet, heat the oil on medium-high heat and sauté the onions and bell peppers till softened.
5. Stir in the beans, Worcestershire sauce, and jalapeño peppers.
6. Reduce the heat to low and simmer, covered for about 5-6 minutes.
7. Split the potatoes and top with the bean mixture.
8. Serve with a sprinkling of the cheese.

Puerto Vallarta
x Houston Meatloaf

🥘 Prep Time: 10 mins
🕐 Total Time: 1 hr 10 mins

Servings per Recipe: 4
Calories	711 kcal
Fat	56.9 g
Carbohydrates	9.8g
Protein	39.2 g
Cholesterol	264 mg
Sodium	1605 mg

Ingredients

1 1/2 lb. ground beef
2 eggs
1 (14.5 oz.) can diced tomatoes with green chili peppers
1 tbsp onion powder
1 tbsp ground black pepper
1 tsp salt

1 slice white bread, cut into cubes
4 slices American cheese

Directions

1. Set your oven to 350 degrees F before doing anything else.
2. In a large bowl, mix together the ground beef, eggs, diced tomatoes and green chili peppers, onion powder, ground black pepper, salt and bread.
3. Transfer the mixture into a 9x5-inch loaf pan and top with the cheese.
4. Cook in the oven for about for about 1 hour.

CHIPOTLE
Burgers

Prep Time: 15 mins
Total Time: 25 mins

Servings per Recipe: 3
Calories   691 kcal
Fat   44.2 g
Carbohydrates   35.4g
Protein   37.3 g
Cholesterol   129 mg
Sodium   1574 mg

Ingredients

1 lb. ground beef
3 tbsp chili seasoning mix
2 chipotle peppers in adobo sauce, minced
1/2 fluid oz. beer
1 chipotle pepper in adobo sauce, minced

1/4 C. mayonnaise
6 (1 oz.) slices white bread
6 (1/2 oz.) slices pepper jack cheese

Directions

1. In a bowl, mix together the ground beef, chili seasoning mix, 2 minced chipotle peppers with adobo sauce, and the beer.
2. Make 3 equal sized patties from the mixture.
3. In a small bowl, mix together the mayonnaise and 1 minced chipotle pepper with adobo sauce.
4. Spread the mayonnaise mixture over the bread slices evenly and top with a slice of pepper jack cheese.
5. Heat a large skillet over medium-high heat and cook the patties for about 5-7 minutes per side.
6. Place 1 burger over 1 slice of the bread and cover with the remaining slices to make sandwiches.
7. Drain the skillet, reserving 2 tbsp of the grease.
8. Heat the reserved grease in the skillet on medium-high heat and cook the sandwiches for about 1-2 minutes per side.

Tex Mex
Seafood Sampler

Prep Time: 15 mins
Total Time: 40 mins

Servings per Recipe: 6
Calories   528 kcal
Fat   14.8 g
Carbohydrates   50.6g
Protein   46.3 g
Cholesterol   232 mg
Sodium   706 mg

Ingredients

1 (16 oz.) package uncooked wide egg noodles
1 tsp olive oil
1 lb. shark steaks, cut into chunks
1 lb. frozen medium shrimp
1 (14.5 oz.) can diced tomatoes and green chilis

2 C. shredded mozzarella cheese
ground black pepper to taste

Directions

1. In a large pan of lightly salted boiling water, cook the egg noodles for about 6 - 8 minutes.
2. Drain well and keep aside.
3. In a bowl, mix together the shark, shrimp, tomatoes and green chilis.
4. In a skillet, heat the olive oil on medium heat and cook the shark mixture, covered for about 15 minutes.
5. Place the shark mixture over the cooked egg noodles and serve with a sprinkling of the mozzarella cheese and pepper.

MEXICAN
Mac n Cheese

Prep Time: 10 mins
Total Time: 30 mins

Servings per Recipe: 6

Calories	384 kcal
Fat	21.1 g
Carbohydrates	27.1g
Protein	19 g
Cholesterol	73 mg
Sodium	784 mg

Ingredients

1 lb. lean ground beef
1 (1.25 oz.) package taco seasoning mix
1 (7.3 oz.) package white Cheddar
macaroni and cheese mix

2 tbsp butter
1/4 C. milk

Directions

1. Heat a large skillet on medium heat and cook the beef till browned completely.
2. Drain the excess grease from the skillet.
3. Add the taco seasoning and water according to seasoning package directions and simmer for about 10 minutes.
4. Remove from the heat and keep aside.
5. Prepare the macaroni and cheese according to package's directions, adding butter and milk as indicated.
6. Add the beef mixture and stir to combine.
7. Serve immediately.

La Paz Corn Soup

Prep Time: 10 mins
Total Time: 40 mins

Servings per Recipe: 6
Calories	299 kcal
Fat	18.6 g
Carbohydrates	29.5g
Protein	8.6 g
Cholesterol	45 mg
Sodium	706 mg

Ingredients

1 1/2 C. chopped onion
2 tbsp margarine
1 tbsp all-purpose flour
1 tbsp chili powder
1 tsp ground cumin
1 (16 oz.) package frozen corn kernels, thawed

2 C. medium salsa
1 (14.5 oz.) can chicken broth
8 oz. cream cheese, softened
1 C. milk

Directions

1. In a large pan, melt the margarine and sauté the onion.
2. Stir in the flour, chili powder and cumin.
3. Add the corn, picante sauce and broth and bring to a boil.
4. Remove from the heat.
5. In a small bowl, add the cream cheese.
6. Gradually add 1/4 C. of the hot mixture into cream cheese and stir to combine well.
7. Add cream cheese mixture and milk into the pan, stirring till well combined and cook till heated completely.
8. Serve immediately.

FORT WORTH
Party Dip

Prep Time: 15 mins
Total Time: 15 mins

Servings per Recipe: 6
Calories	299 kcal
Fat	18.6 g
Carbohydrates	29.5g
Protein	8.6 g
Cholesterol	45 mg
Sodium	706 mg

Ingredients

1 (16 oz.) can refried beans
1 C. guacamole
1/4 C. mayonnaise
1 (8 oz.) container sour cream
1 (1 oz.) package taco seasoning mix
2 C. shredded Cheddar cheese
1 tomato, chopped

1/4 C. chopped green onions
1/4 C. black olives, drained

Directions

1. In a large serving dish, spread the refried beans and top with the guacamole.
2. In a medium bowl, mix together the mayonnaise, sour cream and taco seasoning mix.
3. Spread the mayonnaise mixture over the layer of guacamole evenly, followed by a layer of the Cheddar cheese, tomato, green onions and black olives.

Cajun
Texas Sirloin Burgers

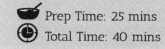 Prep Time: 25 mins

Total Time: 40 mins

Servings per Recipe: 4

Calories	714 kcal
Fat	49.1 g
Carbohydrates	28.5g
Protein	38.3 g
Cholesterol	132 mg
Sodium	1140 mg

Ingredients

1/2 C. mayonnaise
1 tsp Cajun seasoning
1 1/3 lb. ground beef sirloin
1 jalapeno pepper, seeded and chopped
1/2 C. diced white onion
1 clove garlic, minced
1 tbsp Cajun seasoning

1 tsp Worcestershire sauce
4 slices pepper jack cheese
4 hamburger buns, split
4 leaves lettuce
4 slices tomato

Directions

1. Set your grill for medium-high heat and grease the grill grate.
2. In a small bowl, mix together the mayonnaise and 1 tsp of the Cajun seasoning.
3. In a large bowl, add the ground sirloin, jalapeño pepper, onion, garlic, 1 tbsp of the Cajun seasoning and Worcestershire sauce and mix till well combined.
4. Make 4 equal sized patties from the mixture.
5. Cook the patties on the grill for about 5 minutes from both sides.
6. During the last 2 minutes, place a cheese slice over each patty.
7. Spread the seasoned mayonnaise onto the insides of the buns evenly.
8. Arrange the burgers in the buns and top with the lettuce and tomato before serving.

AZTECA
Soup

Prep Time: 20 mins
Total Time: 1 hr 40 mins

Servings per Recipe: 6
Calories	159 kcal
Fat	10.1 g
Carbohydrates	7.4g
Protein	10.5 g
Cholesterol	27 mg
Sodium	43 mg

Ingredients

2 skinless, boneless chicken breast
halves, flattened
3 tbsp olive oil
1 onion, chopped
3 cloves garlic, minced
1 lb. chopped tomatillos
2 jalapeno peppers, seeded and minced
4 C. chicken stock
1/4 tsp cayenne pepper

1/2 tsp hot pepper sauce
2 tbsp chopped fresh cilantro
1/4 C. sour cream (optional)
salt to taste
ground black pepper to taste

Directions

1. In a large pan, heat the oil on high heat and sear the chicken for about 2 minutes per side.
2. Transfer the chicken into a plate and keep aside.
3. In the same pan, add the onions and garlic and sauté till golden.
4. Stir in the tomatillos, jalapeño peppers and broth and bring to a boil.
5. Reduce the heat and simmer, covered for about 15 minutes.
6. In a food processor, add the tomatillo mixture in batches and pulse till smooth.
7. Return the pureed mixture to pan and cook till heated completely.
8. Add the cayenne pepper and hot pepper sauce.
9. Cut the chicken into thin slices and then shred it.
10. Add the shredded chicken, salt and pepper and remove from the heat.
11. Divide the soup into the serving bowls.
12. Stir in the cilantro in each bowl and serve with a dollop of the sour cream.

Authentic
Mexican Salsa Verde

🥣 Prep Time: 10 mins

🕐 Total Time: 25 mins

Servings per Recipe: 8

Calories	24 kcal
Fat	0.6 g
Carbohydrates	4.6g
Protein	0.8 g
Cholesterol	0 mg
Sodium	439 mg

Ingredients

1 lb. tomatillos, husked
1/2 C. finely chopped onion
1 tsp minced garlic
1 serrano chili peppers, minced
2 tbsp chopped cilantro
1 tbsp chopped fresh oregano
1/2 tsp ground cumin

1 1/2 tsp salt
2 C. water

Directions

1. In a pan, add the tomatillos, onion, garlic, chili pepper, cilantro, oregano, cumin, salt and water on high heat and bring to a boil.
2. Reduce the heat to medium-low and simmer for about 10-15 minutes.
3. In a blender, add the tomatillos mixture in batches and pulse till smooth.

EAST LA
Guacamole

Prep Time: 20 mins
Total Time: 25 mins

Servings per Recipe: 24
Calories	48 kcal
Fat	3.8 g
Carbohydrates	3.7g
Protein	0.7 g
Cholesterol	0 mg
Sodium	3 mg

Ingredients

6 fresh tomatillos, husks discarded and tomatillos rinsed
1 white onion, quartered
2 cloves garlic
2 jalapeno peppers, seeded if desired
water, to cover
salt to taste

1/4 C. chopped fresh cilantro
1 tbsp fresh lime juice
3 ripe avocados, halved lengthwise and pitted

Directions

1. In a pan, add the tomatillos, onion, garlic, jalapeño peppers and enough water to cover on medium heat and bring them to a boil.
2. Reduce the heat and simmer for about 5-8 minutes.
3. With a slotted spoon, transfer the tomatillos mixture into a blender in batches and pulse till smooth.
4. Add the salt, cilantro and lime juice and pulse for a few seconds to mix.
5. Scoop out the avocado flesh and transfer into the blender and pulse till well combined.

Summer Evening
Tomato and Fruit Pie

Prep Time: 20 mins
Total Time: 1 hr 25 mins

Servings per Recipe: 8

Calories	470 kcal
Fat	20.2 g
Carbohydrates	70.9g
Protein	4 g
Cholesterol	11 mg
Sodium	266 mg

Ingredients

1 pastry for 9-inch double crust pie
3 C. sliced ripe tomatillos
3 C. sliced strawberries
1/4 C. instant tapioca
1 1/2 C. white sugar

1 tsp lemon juice
3 tbsp butter, sliced

Directions

1. Set your oven to 400 degrees F before doing anything else.
2. Place 1 pie crust into a 9-inch pie dish and gently, press to set.
3. In a bowl, mix together the tomatillos, strawberries, tapioca, sugar and lemon juice.
4. Keep aside for about 15 minutes, stirring occasionally.
5. Place the tomatillo-strawberry mixture into the prepared pie crust and top with the butter slices.
6. Cover the pie with the second pie crust and pinch the edges to seal.
7. Cut the slits into the top crust for ventilation.
8. Arrange the pie onto a baking sheet.
9. Cook in the oven for about 50 minutes.

ZACATECAS
Chicken

Prep Time: 10 mins
Total Time: 30 mins

Servings per Recipe: 4
Calories	487 kcal
Fat	33.7 g
Carbohydrates	7.1g
Protein	37.8 g
Cholesterol	108 mg
Sodium	198 mg

Ingredients

1 (3 1/2) lb. whole chicken, cut into 6
pieces
1 lb. fresh tomatillos, husks removed
2 dried California chili pods
3 dried red chili peppers

2 tbsp olive oil
salt to taste

Directions

1. Set your oven to 350 degrees F before doing anything else.
2. In a small roasting pan, place the tomatillos, California chilies and red chili peppers.
3. Cook in the oven for about 20 minutes, turning occasionally.
4. Remove from the oven and transfer the tomatillo mixture and salt into a food processor and pulse till smooth.
5. In a large skillet, heat the oil on medium-high heat and sear the chicken pieces till golden brown.
6. Stir in the tomatillo mixture.
7. Reduce the heat to medium-low and simmer, covered for about 20-25 minutes.

Super-Hot
Fire Salsa

Prep Time: 10 mins
Total Time: 35 mins

Servings per Recipe: 12
Calories   18 kcal
Fat   0.4 g
Carbohydrates   3.5g
Protein   0.6 g
Cholesterol   0 mg
Sodium   50 mg

Ingredients

1 lb. tomatillos, unhusked
2 serrano chili peppers
2 jalapeno chili peppers
8 pequin chili peppers
4 cloves garlic

1 small whole onion, peeled
1/4 C. chopped cilantro
salt to taste

Directions

1. Heat a dry, cast iron pan on medium-high heat and cook the tomatillos, chilis, garlic cloves and onion till the husks of the tomatillos have blackened and their skins turn translucent, flipping occasionally.
2. Transfer the tomatillo mixture into a bowl and keep aside to cool slightly.
3. Remove the husks from the tomatillos and the stems from the chili peppers.
4. In a food processor, add the tomatillos, chili peppers, cilantro and salt and pulse till desired consistency.
5. Transfer the salsa into a pan on medium heat and cook for about 5 minutes.

LATE SPRING
Tilapia

Prep Time: 25 mins
Total Time: 50 mins

Servings per Recipe: 4

Calories	213 kcal
Fat	7.2 g
Carbohydrates	12.4g
Protein	24.7 g
Cholesterol	41 mg
Sodium	68 mg

Ingredients

cooking spray
1 large red bell pepper, seeds removed
and pepper quartered lengthwise
2 tsp canola oil
1 C. husked, cored and chopped
tomatillos
salt and ground black pepper to taste
1 clove garlic, minced
1/4 C. chopped fresh parsley
2 tbsp rice vinegar
1 tsp honey
2 tbsp all-purpose flour

2 tsp chili powder
1 tsp dried oregano
4 tilapia fillets
2 tsp canola oil
1 lemon, halved and seeds removed
1 sprig fresh cilantro, chopped (optional)

Directions

1. Set the broiler of your oven and arrange oven rack about 6-inches from the heating element.
2. Line a baking sheet with a greased piece of the foil.
3. Arrange the pepper pieces, cut sides down onto the prepared baking sheet.
4. Cook under the broiler for about 5-10 minutes.
5. Transfer the blackened pepper pieces into a bowl.
6. Immediately with a plastic wrap, cover the bowl tightly and keep aside for about 20 minutes.
7. Remove the skins of the pepper pieces and discard.
8. In a large nonstick skillet, heat 2 tsp of the canola oil on medium heat and cook the tomatillos for about 8 minutes.
9. Stir in the salt, black pepper and garlic and cook for about 1 minute.

10. In a blender, add the hot tomatillos, roasted red pepper, parsley, rice vinegar and honey and pulse till smooth.
11. In a shallow bowl, mix together the flour, chili powder, and dried oregano.
12. Season the fish fillets with the salt and black pepper and coat with the flour mixture evenly.
13. In a skillet, heat 2 tsp of the canola oil on medium-high heat and cook the fish fillets for about 2-3 minutes.
14. Carefully flip the side and cook for about 4 minutes.
15. Transfer the fish fillets into a serving platter.
16. Serve with a drizzling of the lemon juice alongside the pan sauce.

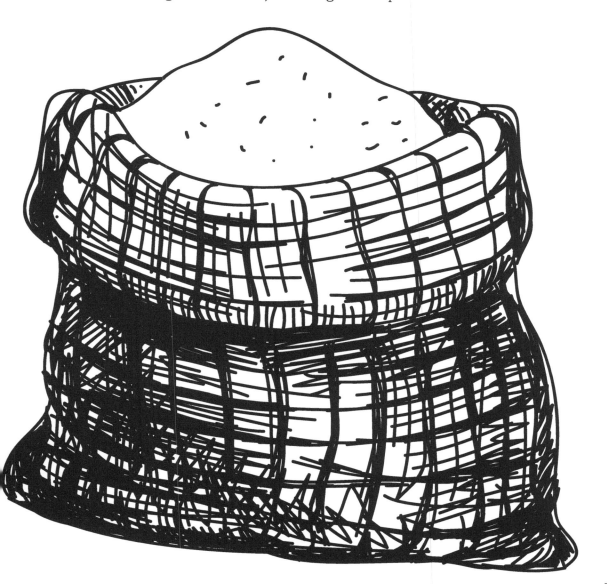

ECUADORIAN
Inspired Chutney

Prep Time: 30 mins
Total Time: 1 hr 45 mins

Servings per Recipe: 25	
Calories	135 kcal
Fat	0.6 g
Carbohydrates	32.8g
Protein	1.3 g
Cholesterol	0 mg
Sodium	61 mg

Ingredients

5 C. chopped green tomatoes
4 C. fresh tomatillos, husked, rinsed, and chopped
1 1/2 C. golden raisins
1 1/2 C. chopped onion
2 1/4 C. packed brown sugar
1/2 tsp salt
1 3/4 C. apple cider vinegar

1 1/2 tbsp pickling spice
1 1/2 tsp chili powder
2 tbsp finely chopped crystallized ginger
1 tbsp brown mustard seed
5 (1 pint) canning jars with lids and rings

Directions

1. In a large pan, add the green tomatoes, tomatillos, raisins, onion, brown sugar, salt, apple cider vinegar, pickling spice, chili powder, crystallized ginger and brown mustard seed on medium heat and bring to a boil.
2. Cook, stirring continuously till the brown sugar is dissolved.
3. Reduce heat and simmer for about 1-2 hours, stirring occasionally.
4. In a pan of boiling water, sterilize the jars and lids for at least 5 minutes.
5. Place the chutney into the hot, sterilized jars, filling the jars to within 1/4-inch of the top.
6. Run a knife around the insides of the jars to remove any air bubbles.
7. With a moist paper towel, wipe the rims of the jars to remove any food residue.
8. Top with the lids and screw on rings.
9. In the bottom of a large pan, arrange a rack and fill halfway with the water.
10. Bring to a boil on high heat.
11. Carefully with a holder, place the jars into the pan, leaving a 2-inch space between the jars.
12. Add more boiling water if necessary till the water level is at least 1-inch above the tops of the jars.

13. Again, bring to a full boil and process, covered for about 15-20 minutes.
14. Remove the jars from the pan and place onto a wood surface, several inches apart to cool completely.
15. After cooling with a finger, press the top of each lid.
16. Store in a cool, dark area.

6-INGREDIENT
Dip

🥣 Prep Time: 10 mins
🕐 Total Time: 15 mins

Servings per Recipe: 8
Calories	92 kcal
Fat	7.7 g
Carbohydrates	6.4g
Protein	1.4 g
Cholesterol	0 mg
Sodium	151 mg

Ingredients

7 oz. fresh tomatillos, husks discarded
and tomatillos rinsed
1/4 C. thickly sliced white onion
1 fresh jalapeno chili
1/2 C. packed fresh cilantro sprigs

2 Hass avocados
1/2 tsp salt

Directions

1. In a small pan, add the tomatillos, onion and jalapeño and enough water to cover and bring to a boil.
2. Cook for about 5 minutes.
3. Drain and run under cold water to stop the cooking, then again drain well.
4. Half the jalapeño lengthwise and scrape out ribs and seeds, then cut into thick slices.
5. In a food processor, add the tomatillo mixture and cilantro and pulse till chopped finely but small chunks remain.
6. Half the avocados lengthwise and discard the pits.
7. Scoop out the flesh and transfer into a bowl.
8. With a fork, mash the avocado and salt till chunky.
9. Fold in the tomatillo mixture and serve.

Easy
Fried Tomatoes

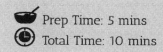 Prep Time: 5 mins

Total Time: 10 mins

Servings per Recipe: 4

Calories	133 kcal
Fat	7.7 g
Carbohydrates	13.4g
Protein	3.4 g
Cholesterol	0 mg
Sodium	256 mg

Ingredients

2 egg white, lightly beaten
1/3 C. cornmeal
1/2 tsp herbs de Provence
1/2 tsp garlic salt
ground black pepper to taste

8 tomatillos, husked and sliced 1/4 inch thick
2 tbsp vegetable oil

Directions

1. In a shallow bowl, add the egg whites.
2. In another shallow bowl, mix together the cornmeal, herbs, salt and pepper.
3. Dip the tomatillo slices in egg whites and then coat with the cornmeal mixture evenly.
4. In a skillet, heat the oil on medium heat and fry the tomatillo slices for about 2-3 minutes per side.
5. Serve immediately.

CINCO DE MAYO
Fajitas

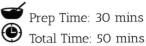 Prep Time: 30 mins
Total Time: 50 mins

Servings per Recipe: 5
Calories	51 kcal
Fat	2.2 g
Carbohydrates	7.8g
Protein	1.7 g
Cholesterol	0 mg
Sodium	5 mg

Ingredients

2 tsp olive oil
2 cloves garlic, minced
2 green bell peppers, sliced
2 yellow bell peppers, sliced
1/2 onion, sliced

1 C. mushrooms, sliced
3 green onions, chopped
lemon pepper to taste

Directions

1. In a large frying pan over a medium heat and sauté the garlic for about 2 minutes.
2. Stir in the green and yellow bell peppers and sauté for about 2 minutes.
3. Stir in the onions and sauté for about 2 minutes.
4. Stir in the mushrooms and green onions and lemon pepper and cook, covered till the vegetables become tender.

American
Fajitas

🥘 Prep Time: 20 mins
🕐 Total Time: 2 hrs 40 mins

Servings per Recipe: 4
Calories   896 kcal
Fat   37.8 g
Carbohydrates   103.9g
Protein   37.8 g
Cholesterol   76 mg
Sodium   1182 mg

Ingredients

1 lb. lean steak, cut into strips
1/2 C. fresh lime juice
1/2 tbsp ground black pepper
1 tbsp chopped fresh cilantro
2 tbsp vegetable oil
1 large onion, cut into thin strips

1 julienned green bell pepper
2 lemons, quartered
salt and pepper to taste
6 (12 inch) flour tortillas

Directions

1. In a shallow dish, mix together the lime juice, ground pepper and cilantro.
2. Add the steak strips and coat with marinade generously.
3. Refrigerate to marinate for about 2-4 hours.
4. In a large skillet, heat 1 tbsp of the vegetable oil on medium-high heat and stir fry the steak strips till desired doneness.
5. Transfer the steak into a plate and keep aside.
6. In the same skillet, heat the remaining oil on medium-low heat and sauté the onions till tender.
7. Stir in the green peppers and steak and the juice of 1 lemon over the top and cook till the green bell peppers are just tender.
8. Remove the pan from the heat and stir in the salt and pepper.
9. Serve the steak fajitas with the tortillas and lemon wedges on the side.

VEGETARIAN
Fajitas

Prep Time: 15 mins
Total Time: 25 mins

Servings per Recipe: 5
Calories	424 kcal
Fat	11.3 g
Carbohydrates	67.4g
Protein	29.7 g
Cholesterol	0 mg
Sodium	924 mg

Ingredients

3 tbsp olive oil
1 red bell pepper, cut into strips
1 green bell pepper, cut into strips
1 yellow bell pepper, cut into strips
1/2 red onion, chopped
1 lb. seitan, cut into strips
2 tbsp reduced-soy sauce

3 cloves garlic, minced
1 tsp chili powder
1 tsp paprika
1 tsp ground cumin
10 whole grain tortillas

Directions

1. In a large skillet, heat the oil on medium heat and sauté the red bell pepper, green bell pepper, yellow bell pepper and onion for about 3-5 minutes.
2. Add the seitan, soy sauce, garlic, chili powder, paprika and cumin and cook for about 7-10 minutes.
3. Place the seitan filling onto each tortilla and fold the tortilla around filling.

Barbeque Party
Fajitas

Prep Time: 20 mins
Total Time: 1 hr

Servings per Recipe: 6

Calories	248 kcal
Fat	16 g
Carbohydrates	5g
Protein	20.4 g
Cholesterol	49 mg
Sodium	44 mg

Ingredients

Marinade:
1/4 C. extra-virgin olive oil
1/2 lime, zested and juiced
2 cloves garlic, minced
1/2 tsp ground cumin
1/4 tsp red pepper flakes
1/4 tsp ground chipotle pepper

1 1/2 lb. beef sirloin, cut into 1-inch cubes
1 red bell pepper, cut into 1-inch cubes
1 green bell pepper, cut into 1-inch cubes
1/2 onion, cut into 1-inch cubes
skewers

Directions

1. In a large glass bowl, add the olive oil, lime juice, lime zest, garlic, cumin, red pepper flakes and chipotle pepper and beat till well combined.
2. Add the sirloin and toss to coat evenly.
3. With a plastic wrap, cover the bowl and refrigerate to marinate for about 30 minutes to 2 hours.
4. Set your outdoor grill for medium-high heat and lightly grease the grill grate.
5. Remove sirloin from the marinade and discard the excess marinade.
6. Thread the sirloin, red bell pepper, green bell pepper and onion onto skewers.
7. Cook on the grill until sirloin for about 4 minutes per side.

CANCUN
Cabin Fajitas

Prep Time: 20 mins
Total Time: 45 mins

Servings per Recipe: 8
Calories	475 kcal
Fat	35.7 g
Carbohydrates	4.6 g
Protein	32.8 g
Cholesterol	104 mg
Sodium	532 mg

Ingredients

3 lb. beef skirt steak
3 tsp garlic powder
3 tsp fajita seasoning
8 slices bacon
1 onion, chopped
1 bell pepper, chopped
1/2 bunch cilantro, chopped

1 large tomato, chopped
10 oz. shredded Monterey Jack cheese

Directions

1. Rub the steaks with the garlic powder and fajita seasoning evenly.
2. Cut the steaks into 1 1/2-inch strips and keep aside.
3. Heat a large skillet on medium heat and cook the bacon till just crisp and brown.
4. Stir in the chopped onion, bell pepper, cilantro and steak strips and cook, stirring occasionally for about 7 minutes.
5. Stir in the tomatoes and cook till heated through.
6. Remove from the heat and serve with a topping of the Monterey Jack cheese.

Ethan's
Favorite Fajitas

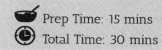
Prep Time: 15 mins
Total Time: 30 mins

Servings per Recipe: 10	
Calories	427 kcal
Fat	10.3 g
Carbohydrates	64.2g
Protein	18 g
Cholesterol	21 mg
Sodium	1078 mg

Ingredients

2 green bell peppers, sliced
1 red bell pepper, sliced
1 onion, thinly sliced
1 C. fresh sliced mushrooms
2 C. diced, cooked chicken meat
1 (.7 oz.) package dry Italian-style salad dressing mix

10 (12 inch) flour tortillas

Directions

1. Cut the peppers and onion into thin slices lengthwise.
2. Heat a greased skillet on low heat and sauté the peppers and onion till tender.
3. Add mushrooms and chicken and cook till heated completely.
4. Stir in the dry salad dressing mix and mix completely.
5. Warm the tortillas and roll the mixture inside.
6. If desired top with the shredded cheddar cheese, diced tomato and shredded lettuce.

VEGAN
Fajitas

 Prep Time: 10 mins
Total Time: 25 mins

Servings per Recipe: 4
Calories	207 kcal
Fat	13.3 g
Carbohydrates	13.2g
Protein	12.8 g
Cholesterol	0 mg
Sodium	606 mg

Ingredients

2 tbsp corn oil
1 (8 oz.) package tempeh, broken into
bite-sized pieces
2 tbsp soy sauce
1 1/2 C. chopped green bell pepper
1 (4.5 oz.) can sliced mushrooms,
drained

1 tbsp lime juice
1/2 C. frozen chopped spinach, thawed
and drained
1 tbsp chopped green chili peppers
1 tbsp chopped fresh cilantro
1 tbsp dried minced onion

Directions

1. In a large skillet, heat the oil on medium heat and sauté the tempeh with the soy sauce and lime juice till the tempeh browns.
2. Stir in the bell peppers, mushrooms, spinach, chili peppers, cilantro and dried onion and increase the heat to medium-high.
3. Cook, stirring occasionally till the liquid has reduced.

ENJOY THE RECIPES?
KEEP ON COOKING
WITH 6 MORE FREE COOKBOOKS!

Visit our website and simply enter your email address to join the club and receive your 6 cookbooks.

http://booksumo.com/magnet

https://www.instagram.com/booksumopress/

https://www.facebook.com/booksumo/

Printed in Great Britain
by Amazon